As you read, you can feel the energy and pain, yet also the warm presence of my mom's growth as an individual in her writing. She helps bring out strengths, dreams, and visions as you peel back the layers while figuring out who you really are. Being able to reflect and share in a space right alongside her results in healing and discovery on the journey to be your true authentic self.
—*Brandee Ramseur, Finance Director at Brotherton Cadillac*

Kerri-Elizabeth Lohrey's writing is indeed righting. I experienced the power of the pen in her book *Write It*. Her gift transported me to the depths of my soul by putting the wheel of my journey in my own hands. Her writing inspired me to unearth hidden pains and joys previously buried so that I could right my own ship. An experience I can only describe through her writing:

In the details an image is created Reflection is stated

In wonder we are inspired

Listen to the vibration

The living breath of creation

Read it, and you will right it. Experience the reflection, the wonder, and the vibration of your own living breath of creation in Kerri-Elizabeth Lohrey's exquisitely written book *Write It*.
—*Marlowe T. Brown*
Co-founder, Regeneration Institute, LLC

As a result of turning to nature for answers through the highs and lows of her own life experiences, Kerri has acquired a rich wisdom that has been distilled poetically in this small volume. With space between each verse, she invites you to embrace the fullness of your own journey, and write it!
—*Austin Broadbent owner/ Sweet Sage Coffee Co.*

Write It

Kerri-Elizabeth

Published by
Hybrid Global Publishing
333 E 14th Street
#3C
New York, NY 10003

Manufactured in the United States of America, or in the United Kingdom when distributed elsewhere.

Lohrey, Kerri-Elizabeth.
Write It
        ISBN: 978-1-961757-30-1
        LCCN: 2023923303

Cover design by: Kerri Elizabeth; Joe Potter
Copyediting by: Creative Editorial Solutions
Interior design by: Creative Editorial Solutions

Kerri-Elizabeth.com

DEDICATION

To my son, "Zakary," for showing me the blessings of perseverance through our always-changing present circumstances. Thank you for trusting me to be your mom and courageously entering life with determination and fire under your feet—and twenty-four-plus years later teaching me that we are only here temporarily, and it is up to us how we live it, share it, teach it, and experience it. Thank you for the depth you shared with me on your journey through this life in the physical form, and thank you for teaching me and showing me "that" you are never gone.

Born October 31, 1992, and forever living and teaching me to "write" my way to love, live, breathe, express, be heard, dream, persevere, inspire, grow, be kind, trust myself and the process, be persistent, aware, listen, learn, give, and receive.

CONTENTS

MEET THE AUTHOR

Kerri-Elizabeth is first a woman on a courageously driven journey to self-improvement while experiencing the challenges of life that she explains as "happening for her, so she can meet more of herself and give a better version each day to herself and others."

She is a woman in her own "rights" (WRITES) that has stripped down the titles of her life to tap into the deeper, more aware, and untamed inner self.

She has titles that life has gifted her through education that is always evolving and growing, although these gifts and amazing experiences do not define her or her purpose. She goes deeper, and now she is offering YOU a gift to journey on your path to the most important part of all you will ever do—and that is "You," a place where all solutions reside, just waiting for you to notice.

Walk into life's experiences, continually learning to observe rather than judge, listen rather than take it personally, and ask yourself continually, "What part of me is affected for good or for otherwise . . . and why? Then WRITE IT.

This will lead you to the "WRITE" to love, live, laugh, dream, be heard, listen, adventure, let go, go deeper into the solution, express anger, hurt, open wounds that have healed shut before the trauma has been released, enter with courage, consistency, and awareness, and most of all, enter with trust in yourself. The path is not easy. It doesn't show up without pain. It didn't get there without pain, but it will also show up with excitement and inspiration, and it will gift you an opportunity to meet more of you. And you're worth it!

INTRODUCTION

Courage is more than "you want to" and stronger than your "need to." It is the part of you you'll never know unless you "choose to."

Welcome to this space created especially for growth where you can read inspiring words and write what part of you is inspired and why. Each of you will find your pace and purpose within this interactive space built to inspire places and spaces within you that will grow you and teach you and show you that you have all the solutions within you.

This is a tool for you to express more of YOU and what you want in your life. It all happens with you, no matter who nudges you or teaches you, who holds you, who loves you. No matter what the circumstances are, the traumas and the trials, the goals and the dreams, you are the only one that can take the action needed for your inner change. You are the solution, and action is your choice.

I am more than what
I thought defined me!

YOU ARE MORE

I am more than the child that grew up with
fight-or-flight emotions and feelings
An imposter lived here, a fearful, unready,
and unwilling part of me
In control of nothing but wanting to control everything
Living in a darkness of the world
Running into it at the same time
I was running away from it
Religion captured me and gave me
a safe box to live in for years
Oh, God is very real to me,
but religion is no longer a vice
That box got smaller as experiences got bigger,
and it didn't make sense to live there anymore
I couldn't breathe
I couldn't talk
I couldn't move
I couldn't escape the judgment of
what I was told I needed to do and not
what my deeper self was calling me to do
I was screaming inside for years
As if I were watching myself from a distance,
I observed so much confusion and pain

Filled with insecurities grounded in shame and blame
that I could never do enough to erase
What I faced was the habit in my energy
The energy that was continually lived in fight-or-flight,
overcompensations, under-compensations,
and so much more
While smiling and living I was also dying
I was raising kids while raising myself
I was married while not even
understanding what that required
I lived small because small seemed bigger than
what I felt capable of handling at times
I lived on others' terms because I had no idea
life had terms I had the power to make
I knew deep within there was more
I knew deep within I had more
I chose more of myself too many times than to allow
doubt to loosen my grip
I had no idea how to break through to that next place
Disappointing others while listening to my own calling
was like climbing Mt. Everest with no training
That's when I realized it was going to mean I had to
disappoint myself
It all required me to retrain myself
I had to change my story, and I was going to have to
reject the current narrative and disappoint myself
by announcing I was more than the skin
I had lived in all these years
That would seem like a milestone in gratitude to many;
however, it meant to me that I had to invite part of myself

to move out
I had to leave behind the blame, the shame,
and the rejections—not just of my own but from others
I now could give myself safety
I now could stand strong for me
I could say I mattered
I could say NO
I now could disappoint another to show up for myself,
knowing that the disappointment was their journey
and I had no business fixing it
I had to thank the space and move away,
bless it for the experiences and lessons,
and leave it behind
It wasn't supposed to become me—
it was suppose to teach me
It did
At the exact time it was supposed to
It happened in loss
It happened in change
It happened in pain
It happened in tears
It didn't happen with joy or laughter
It happened when I felt no hope
It happened when I was empty
When I was my most challenged
It happened in anger
In rejections
It happened in misunderstandings I had to let go of
and allow the teaching of it
It happened in letting go of people

I thought would never leave
It happened in learning how to have a relationship
with my son from the heavens
instead of in the physical presence
It happened in sickness
It happened in the lowest times, the hardest times,
the most doubtful times
It is still happening, and I understand that
these times are never to be wished away
but to be observed with new insight
To look into pain and to ache while you smile is part of
life's best and most insightful journeys to success
Happiness is a foundation that requires remodeling
continually

WRITE IT

WRITE IT

WRITE IT

It will be up to you to venture through the gaps in time where change is waiting.

GAPS IN TIME

A new beginning . . . the choice is available daily
However, often it is saved for the beginning of a new year
The past has fallen away as you have slept
and dreamed yourself into the present
May your dreams waiting to be fulfilled have
a clear path to so many grand tomorrows
Allow forgiveness to thrive within your heart
with valuable insights
An invitation from the core of a happy, peaceful existence
meets you face-to-face
Honor your deepest growth and spend moments
under the stars and chasing waterfalls
Let go of the "what and who was" to see
your brightest days
Often the pain of letting go comes with what we think
others will feel by our changes
Growth is a choice for all, and you will never
please everyone — and often not even the
ones you intend to please most
Keep growing anyway . . .
that's where your strongest self is

WRITE IT

WRITE IT

Where moments of awareness
exist, curiosity teaches.

DEPTH OF REFLECTION

Is the depth of a reflection upon water infinite?
Where does it start?
Where does it extend?
Upon a breeze, an unsteadiness gives a blur
Calm pristine duplication in the reflection recovers
Steadiness reserves itself
Offering peace to a storm
Sunshine arrives with rain upon its rays
An open sky seems to smile upon the waters
Leaving curiosity to dance upon the moment
Where does it start?
Where does it extend?
Where pristine is duplicated in a reflection
Love is moved within the awareness
Where does it start?
Where does it extend?
Rain dances with the sun
Beauty of a moment arrives
Awareness in every breath takes place
Love is in the rays
Love is in the ripples of the water upon a whisper of wind
Love is in the rain asking for the hand of every sunshine rays
Love is
Where it starts
Where it extends
Within

WRITE IT

WRITE IT

Whether separate or connected, both become defined purely by experience and emotion.

SEPARATELY FOUND
WHILE ALWAYS CONNECTED

Present in the connection
River roaring to its chosen audience
Birds performing a soul-moving orchestra
Trees adding their own rhythm practiced daily
with precision
While the breeze so eloquently smooths every tune
into an inner song
All echoing from the majestic mountains
offering a priceless concert
An invitation is not needed
A willingness to enter is
Intense scents of pine inspire your deepest senses
Sweetly journeying through every fiber of pain
transforming it into gratitude
Resting freely atop one of nature's strengths
Love and connection are found
Separate and clearly joined
Birds sing to one another as if love is all that really exists
Is it . . .
The sound of the river takes no space
Instead joyfully takes ownership of its existence

to nurture presence
It carries wounds down that never return
It erases hardship without asking
The aroma of the river and pine create a tea
for you and nature to thrive upon
Each needle left upon the ground leaving
a legacy of its time here
Burn marks upon the trees carry a wisdom
into healing and regeneration

WRITE IT

WRITE IT

WRITE IT

Within the clouds, intention and focus are highlighted for your success.

WITHIN THE CLOUDS

Sometimes the seemingly hardest times
offer the most pivotal changes
Hunger for the deepest truths drives a
relentless anxiety to know more
Deeply falling apart coordinates with a rising again
Disappearing into sacrifice opens transformation
Change must persevere while ripples of time disappear
Explanation is not apparent
An inner peace is sacrificed to enter through the clouds
You must purely trust the navigation system studied
Rising above the clouds dances with pure intention
Focus cannot be lost
It is within the cloud you will question your strengths
It is above the clouds you will be
reminded of your strengths
Never to forget
Once you are above the clouds, you must return
Again you will question your strengths
Again you will be reminded who you are
Fall apart into who you are meant to be
The fall is part of the rising
The rising is part of the fall
The clouds are where intention and focus is planted

WRITE IT

WRITE IT

Observation from the heart gives
perspective to the mind and vision
to new insight.

OBSERVE

Pouring down rain was calling her name
The thunder was rolling, her heart consoling, the rain was
calling her in
The drops were flowing and the wind was blowing
She heard it, and it called her in
The freedom in the rain silenced any pain
It was still calling her in
Her clothes were soaked, her curls were gone, drops of
water dripped from her head
The puddle below was a gift to grow
It reflected an amazing glow
She stood outside for hours and hours, dancing to the
sound of the rain
Every drop was amazing, she couldn't get enough
It kept calling her out of the pain
A hand reached out and said, "MOM, let's jump and be
glad for the puddle-stomping game"
They jumped and they jumped and splashed and laughed
They giggled and had a blast
Now when it rains, it reflects, letting go of the pain
The days and years go by
The moments pass before your eyes
Is your heart in the game or do you stay tame?
Let go and have fun, jump in the mud
Your life has truly just begun

WRITE IT

WRITE IT

.

When stillness awakens,
it will be movement that creates
your story!

LANGUAGE IN THE HILLS

The wind searches for the grass and dances shamelessly
Awakening all stillness
Ripples upon the river speak volumes
Canyons yearn for the echo of a voice
Flowers are sprouting among the spring
Blades of grass, yellow and green, arise from the hills
Sunshine widens every horizon with hope,
showing nature's beauty
Nothing is missing; complete serenity exists
Fulfillment is within the winds, flowers, the grass,
and the brisk breeze
Language is within nature's presence and
existence is peaceful
Majestic hills speak volumes while the river
kisses every curve
Trees with wisdom share a melody
When at the top of the hill

WRITE IT

WRITE IT

Perspective shows you it is purely where you stand where love blooms.

COMPLACENT SURPRISE

Complacency will sneak a surprise
Views will be challenged and priority changes
Adaption will trickle through asking to be settled in
Reaction is abrupt and sly, waiting for your awareness
When senses are aware, reaction retreats
Emotion often stretches ahead, and reaction is lured by
the seduction of emotion
Stillness will speak while flirting with
impatience and frustration
Love and awareness play chess with the opponents
Flesh is to be observed when grace is your foundation
It will ultimately be the surrender of action that leads to
your most valued awareness

WRITE IT

WRITE IT

Discipline is choosing between what you want now and what you want most, with strength-building consistency and perseverance to arrive while planning new heights!

COMPONENT

Wake up and start the day
Decide the night before how you will plan the way
Organize the space you're in
So creative thinking can move again
Honor what you planned
Stay focused and make a stand
If you need help, don't hesitate to ask
It is important to complete the task
Are you having a debate
Are you stuck in past mistakes
Are you looking for a plan to work out
Are you procrastinating and checked out
Do you wake up every day excited to
have another chance
You have been gifted that in advance
Remember, your life deserves more than a glance
Today you can make a choice to listen to your inner voice
Today you can make a decision to put down the things
that don't serve your vision
You're worth every moment
Are you missing that component?

WRITE IT

WRITE IT

The battle is up to you—
the war is within you!

OBSERVATION

There will be a love you can't explain
A loss you'll have to navigate through
There will be joy in abundance
Choice will shake and shutter your courage
Investigate strategies of the heart
Feel the silence in the art
Create a way to where no words are forced
Where flow is adapted with grace
May the quiet moments of loss strengthen, not sabotage
Whispers will ride on every thought
Delivering calmness into the light
Mediate your emotions and allow grace and character
to recite wisdom
Believe in the most beautiful miracles
Existence is not to be submissive

WRITE IT

WRITE IT

I want to be the reason you look down at your phone and smile, then accidentally walk into a pole.

SHARE THE LOVE

Laugh until your cheeks hurt
Give
A hug
A smile
A wink
An embrace
A look
A laugh
A giggle
In place
Don't miss it
Don't hide it
Don't let it get by you
Share it
Be there with it
Enjoy it
Delight in it
Be happy you are part of it
Deliver it
Send it
Mend it
Keep it
Own it

Take it
Give it
Receive it
Feel it
Share it
Never let go of it
Be the sunshine in someone's day
and let someone else's sunshine come your way!
Create some fun in your day
Send laughter in many ways!

WRITE IT

WRITE IT

WRITE IT

Every flower holds the petals until the petals let go!

SACRED CHANGE

True sacrifice is within yourself
Acquiesced process of true wealth
Accountable in your unwavering truth
Standing in spiritual flow
Allowing obstructions to be moved to
empower you in growth
The umbilical cord, created for a mother to give life
Then cut to release your purpose to take flight
Birthed from an inner, embracing place
Offered into opportunity to share life in a larger place
Life sheds and rejuvenates the encompassing
presence of ourselves
Revealing integration of our TRUTH
Losing our ego-self to our highest and
most supreme love
Love is shown to be limitless when every
circumstance represents gratitude
Love does not come and go but is obstructed only by
what we know

WRITE IT

WRITE IT

Beyond presence is a surrendering
of offense and defense to be
navigated and inspired to love and
create order.

SACRED EMBRACE

The sacred journey of your soul
Feel into the graceful pull
Let go to what is already set in place
Melt into the cosmic arrangement of space
Divine love is determined for you to embrace
Creation of the ocean's mystery
The heart's authenticity
The Milky Way dancing to adoration
Your body's formation
The mind's intriguing ability to feel
Interpretation to reveal
Listening to the embodiment of being still

WRITE IT

WRITE IT

Embrace the sacred space where
your heart pulls you into place!

SIGNIFICANT SURRENDER

Significantly silent in solitude
Conscious awakening exploding from my soul
Bursting forth the capacity to live more
Deeper in love with this peaceful, open door
Momentum coursing forth
A pace leads to a sacred way to breathe
Swirling and whirling the heart's design
Allowance to be and feel all that's inside of me
Escaping with unrivaled, infinite love
Lessons and gifts molded into treasures of time
Smoothing edges and defining lines
Entering through wounded spaces
Surrendering to open places
Never dimming the purpose to shine bright
Fall into the power of the full moon's night
Align yourself to fall together not apart
Pour rest and reassurance as fuel to restart
Embrace the resuscitation
Breathe out frustration
Graciously invest in your soul's voice
The stage is presented and the microphone on
The echo in a universe recording a song

WRITE IT

WRITE IT

Surrender to the still silence
to hear more!

BEAUTIFUL SOUL

The vines know their route
Beauty added to the view they surround
Tangled only to perception shaken around
Reaching for the stars, never tied or bound
Shooting stars represent core freedom found
Investigating the inner sounds
The sight
The light
The vibrations in the ground
The breathing and pulse of every tree standing proud
Others fallen with a purpose to lay down
Solidity exists firmly untethered by a slippery slope
Polarity is the sun ray's reflection of hope
Rain divinely drops clearing the fog over illusions
Trusting in the strength put into the making of
your own braided twine
Made from the heart and soul when aligned
In a flash blinded but harnessed in alignment

WRITE IT

WRITE IT

The heart and soul will find their place; wounds will heal where sorrow once was in that space!

A FIELD OF FOREVER

Capturing the essence of beauty
Strength in the bend and sway created by a slight breeze
Colors of pure sunlight with a drop of earthly wonder
create a center
Curiosity to grow manifests existence and courage,
reaching for the sky unwavering
A seedling miraculously flourishing as a flower
A flower encompassing the essence of possibilities
Fueling possibility, inspiring optimism
Access infinite evolution
Offer only the presence of your light
Allow the tears to interpret without judgment
And your heart to hear your purpose
Get lost in a field of forever
Plow out the judgments of whys and hows
And water the freedom to love and change
Love is without time and space with a flowing of nothing
Erased and everything at the universe's pace

WRITE IT

WRITE IT

The difference between NOW and LATER will determine the outcome of your goals!

IGNITE IN THE REFLECTION OF LIGHT

It is in the silence I hear you call
It is in the stillness when I finally fall
It is in the shadow reaching abundantly tall
It is in the morning calmness flowing through my veins
The echoing presence where time remains
A cellular turbulence where the sparks ignite a flame
Stay awake and aware to the feeling you bare
Tell me, feeling, where will you take me,
what will you share
Respectfully I honor your presence to care
An elegance of the sun rising in pure captivation
The afternoon glistening, a moment in the gap
The simplicity of an awakened soul on tap
Integrating harmony stitched between the sun and moon
Swimming through the reflections in the lake
Enlightenment surrounds you with no mistake

WRITE IT

WRITE IT

It is when you realize
all attachments to emotions
are like rain.

RAINDROPS

An expression
Unmixed with thoughts
Purely emotion surrendering
Concentrated attention
Immersed in awareness
Behold my heart
Hijack my pain
Turn it into rain
And may that lake
Be named . . . Gratitude

WRITE IT

WRITE IT

The lesson in the reflection is not seen but heard; it is hidden in the silence of your words!

ACCOUNTABILITY FRAMED

Find the fuel that sparks a flame
Release all blame
Jump where you'd rather stand
Standing after falling apart became part of the plan
Cry where tears need space
Create where loneliness resides
Love where doubt pushes you aside
Scream out loud to the full moon
Release the strings not tuned
Emptiness is a place
Where a gift is placed
A surrendered but not-yet-captured infinity
Paint your design with the brush of choice
Framing in the empty space
Where light tunnels through to touch
a deeper part of you

WRITE IT

WRITE IT

Design your plan to stand. While mistakes will be made, the lessons are the courage to maintain accountability to build a solid frame!

THE PATH

May there be love on every path
May calmness be the center at last
May every breath fill your lungs without fail
May that rush of fear pass with a centered exhale
Release and explore the open door
The light inside will show you more
Be still and visualize
Feel and realize
Inside your human space
Embedded into your cellular place
Is love for you to embrace

WRITE IT

WRITE IT

The path you conceive is where your belief is made!

STEP INSIDE WEAKNESS

Energy in the aftermath
Laid upon the earth
Resting for another burst
Stand strong where weakness hurts
Step into it and receive the vulnerability
The direction and possibility
The surge that's shaking you
Weakness is alive when you step inside
To face the fears one at a time

WRITE IT

WRITE IT

Weakness, when tapped into, can give you your greatest strengths.

INFINITY

Do you know anyone up there
Do you ever just daydream
Staring in the sky
Wondering how and why
Do you ever just imagine you can fly
That clouds were magic carpet rides
Have you ever thought about the details in . . . infinity
Infinite, never-ending
More than anything within pages or walls
How could life possibly end
When infinity says, "I'm here, there is no end,
You just fall down and stand up again"
While the spirit soars, infinitely
With no end
Infinity offers the opportunity to stand up
and begin again

WRITE IT

WRITE IT

Life has been determined by humans to start and end, but infinity doesn't end, so stand up and begin again.

IS THAT YOU?

Stretching your limbs
Below the sun's rays
Watch your shadow appear
A distortion of reality
So clear
But is it you
Magnified in this view
So different
Than the reflection in a mirror
Which one are you
The reflection on the water
The shadow on earth
Or the soul observing
How do you view

WRITE IT

WRITE IT

Nature projects different views for you to adventure through. Those views were not set in place to be a judgment of person or place but an adventure through your most inner sacred space.

UNEXPECTED SOUL CONNECTION

Our eyes locked
I feel you
You already know my heart
You don't miss a word
Even a whisper and I'm heard
I'm here
Night arrives
I hear you call
You know I'm near
You've helped me breathe
Your love frees me
We're here
Heart talks
Stillness
You don't rush me
I don't rush you
We arrive daily to this space
Healing is embraced
Anxiety is erased
Somehow you just know my pace
Easing me into the most peaceful place

WRITE IT

WRITE IT

Love through the soul is the most moving love to know!

LOVE ME, LOVE ME NOT

Love me
Love me not
Love me
Love me not
Nature's love shows
When one goes
Another grows
Could it be the daisy has set me free
Love me
Love me not
Nature's love
Always lands on
Love me
A LOT!

WRITE IT

WRITE IT

Walk a path that reflects the capacity of growth and love that honors a courageous legacy.

THE PATH OF LESS RESISTANCE

A photo captured by an inspired eye
Another face, a lens, a voice, a triggered thought
A reflection of perceptual time caught
A heart, a hand, a soul and a creative giver
A moment is captured and, with a blink, it's forever
While moments pass into history
Gestures of inspiration are tattooed into the universe
An alignment of emotion and action snap into a visual
canvas of inspired reality
Memories visually etched into a frame
Viewed in sight yet reflecting personal emotion
The journey of emotion is the true creation
of the visual captured
While a photograph gifts us a captured moment, it's the
eye that gives you the memory
While a photograph captures the visual perception, it's
your inspired memory creating the captured reality

WRITE IT

WRITE IT

There will be seasons and
emotions that create the beauty of
your interpretations.

TO LOVE

To love is to live
To breathe
To share
Believe
Trust
Love
Feel
Encourage
Smile
Delight
Rejoice
To love is to live
You will cry
You will experience fear
Loss
Pain
Doubt
Discouragement
Frustration
It will be your interpretation that determines your outlook.
To love is to embrace these seasons of change and create
a canvas of colorful experiences that will magnify the
power of LOVE!

WRITE IT

WRITE IT

We are all connected to a purposeful living, but we don't all purposefully live.

PURPOSEFULLY CONNECTED

In the midst of the rain, rays of joy appear
In those rays of joy, there is a connection to sorrow
Sorrow is a path that leads to healing
In pain there's an abundance of strength
In strength there's fervent perseverance
In perseverance there's a transparent purpose
In purpose there's solid priority
Priority fuels dedication
In dedication there's unquestioned loyalty
In loyalty there's trusted commitment
In commitment there's unconditional belief
In belief there's infinitely forever
In forever there's infinitely untouched possibilities
Possibilities create encouragement
Encouragement leads to action
Action leads to freedom
Freedom is thriving
In thriving we let go of simply surviving and surrender to
living our purpose

WRITE IT

WRITE IT

When the ground shakes and the sky's awake, stand and be embraced.

SWIRLING INFINITELY

It's safety in this place
It's peace when nature touches your feet
It's a release when the sky opens its blue eyes
It's meditating on the sounds of real times
It's love swirling infinitely with no lines
In the twinkle of natures eyes, you'll find depth
In the wrinkles of a face, embrace the history placed
In a hug there's acceptance
In a glance appears perception
In a heart there are beats
In the soul there's nothing that can compete
When the soul is free, the heart and mind are one beat
Free your soul
Let go of control
Evolve without defeat to arise to your feet
Hear the sounds of real times
See the abstract colors of nature's blended lines
Open the box of limits
And chat with possibilities
Capture carefully the memories of yesterday
While ascending into intentional living, now

WRITE IT

WRITE IT

Don't miss the light of day living someone else's way.

LIGHT OF DAY WILL FADE

When the light of the day slowly fades
Sounds quiet down all around
Shade takes the stage gently
Perspective is changed
Where a moment ago light and shade both took center
stage
They bow with the honor of true love in a universal
exchange
Miraculously the tides never hide
Crashing and surging to a universal rhythm
Pebbles in infinite amounts toss and turn
Offering an insurmountable melody of beauty to align with
Give way to a thought of what is life about
Some days will interpret as heavy
Some say, ready
Others seem even and steady
As the light will slowly fade
Another day is gifted into the nightshade

WRITE IT

WRITE IT

It's in the details that we experience wonder!

IN THE DETAILS

In the details an image is created
Reflection is stated
In wonder we are inspired
Listen to the vibration
The living breath of creation
Stay and pray
Answers will wake you
They may shake you
They may disappoint you
They may leave out details
Persevere
Answers are in the details of creations reflection

WRITE IT

WRITE IT

It is within grace that we are defined and secure; it is within love that healing replaces our scars.

SILENCE

Situations will challenge your pace
People will stretch your capacity and space
Your faith will balance you in this place
Defense will rear its playful head
These are the times that silence is where you tread
Everyone's actions and voice tell a story in time
You can choose to tell it with love
You can choose to tell it with any emotion but love
However, when the story is told
It will reflect the heart space we hold

WRITE IT

WRITE IT

The tides roll in and they roll out, but they never come back exactly the same!

STUBBORN EMBRACE

Tides change inevitably
The sun rises into a sunset
Love and pain
Do they rise and set as well
Life and death, are they lovers
Are we dying to live or living to die
Resistance thrives in our stubborn embrace
Is it resistance that creates our pain
What used to be community has taken on separation
Our younger generation standing for their truth
The older generation standing for theirs
In between a generation split
WAIT!!!
Compassion has no judgments
It doesn't split from itself
It is love' it leads and follows in harmony with our heart
It changes without judgments attached
But instead evolves with understanding

WRITE IT

WRITE IT

Love is the falling apart and coming together in life and never becoming bitter but instead gaining a deeper love for every experience.

THE FALLING APART

Inevitably things fall apart
Preparing a new start
You learn that kindness has a time limit
That love does not promise
Instead the promise is love
You learn moments live in the experience
That experiences are always passing
You learn that light is always available
Even in the dark
You learn that reflection has nothing to do with a mirror
That admission to your life is already paid
You just have to enter, in full presence

WRITE IT

WRITE IT

It is when you realize that all attachments to emotions are like rain.

RAINDROPS

Within every raindrop a mystery
Power in a raindrop creates history
Anticipation of more appears
Raindrops enter like heaven's tears
Cleansing all that's near
How many are there
Where did they hide
Is there matter attached inside
How does condensation appear
With weather, with temperature, with the clouds near
Why don't the clouds fall down
Does a raindrop feel the ground
Raindrops inspiring curiosity and wonder
Often joined by sunshine and thunder
Watering the earth
Filling the lakes
Provoking inspiration through God's grace

WRITE IT

WRITE IT

A path of presence is identified
by the moments you feel your
experience.

SCARS

A path of presence
Resides inside
Waiting to be felt
Alert and aware
Do you dare
Feel the scars you bare
By sight you may see
Scars on every leaf
Scars upon the trees
By sight you may see
Scars upon a cheek
Scars mistaking us as visually weak
Every scar will leave a story
An experience bared
Healing to share
Nature reveals the dance
Along every path
Beyond a glance
Scars reveal another chance

WRITE IT

WRITE IT

Embracing the moments of change teaches wisdom in place of resistance and fear.

PIVOTAL MOMENTS

Moments that seem to stop time
Moments where everything aligns
Gentleness and compassion intertwined
Letting go and holding on don't exist
Presence is perfect
Where streams and rivers run free
Crossing paths with eternity
Then like a tree that falls across the river flow
Forcing a new direction
Beauty of change erupts the soul
Flow is held for a moment
Time is stopped
Panic and anxiety whisper nonsense to fear
Then so clear compassion gently taps
I'm here

WRITE IT

WRITE IT

Growth takes a lifetime of strength through every season—don't miss a drop of rain or a ray of sunshine.

WHISPER YOUR STORY

Whisper to me your journey to the sky
Speak slowly so I can write them all
Share with me every raindrop you've felt
Every shiver in the storms
As you stand protecting me
Share with me every ring you earned at your core
As you share, I'm listening
To the winds shuffling your leaves
The crackling among your branches
The dew among the grass sharing precious reflections
May nature always inspire in you growth
Where God so creatively painted all the answers

WRITE IT

WRITE IT

Keep your chords in tune
continually; allow the tunes to
change and a song to play!

MOMENTS TUNE THE CHORDS

In the chords of an inner vibration, a song plays
A beautiful song narrated with a personal commitment to
live unconditionally in love
A dare to live bravely with honesty beyond a normal
comprehension
To live without the bondage of judgments, but listen to
honor my own reflective growth
To love what is idealized as good and bad and consume
the varied possibilities of perception
This song evolves and cultivates the depth of goodness
Music erupts from the strings that pull my heart
The surge of beats echoes through the halls
of this fiercely built soul
Instrumental notes play in random order, sharing
their part in the song
Mind and body create a bass beat in the background,
rumbling and consuming core strength
Tranquility and unity empathize with the suffering
sound of pain
Healing must occur through the releasing
of anything other than love
Change takes a path and tunes in the sound, creating
meditations carrying this moment

WRITE IT

WRITE IT

Find peace in nature's house;
it will show you what life's about.

REFLECTIONS IN THE DEW

The fire's up and crackling with noise
The morning is starting with nature's poise
The birds are singing gratitude to the young and old
The sun is rising with colors of gold
The air is crisp, delivering a kiss
The mountain's posture is nothing but bliss
The blanket covering the blue sky chose
a different direction to fly
The raindrops falling off the tree sparkle with
a reflection of all it can see
An evening rain came through
Massaging every tree limb, leaving mirror drops of dew
In the far distance, different callings through the trees
Nature is waking with thoughts to please
Breathe in the beauty of what is real
Breathe in the calmness entering your heart to reveal
Keep the magnificent harmony inside
Peace is given; it's not hard to find
Tap into your soul; it knows the way
It's consistent and loving every day
What do you want in life today
Choose your path in all you say
Look in the reflection of the raindrops' dew
They're placed perfectly to show you
Sun shining on your day
Your soul has more to say

WRITE IT

WRITE IT

Loving you in all you do, forgiving you and moving through, learning to be more of you, in all you do there is one direction to follow through, YOU.

LOVING YOU

Loving you.
When the sky is blue, I see you.
When the grass is filled with a green tone too,
I'm loving you.
When the silence is clear,
When all I hear is nature's voice near,
I'm loving you.
When the sun shines on my face,
When my heart enters a race,
I'm loving you.
When the rain is pouring,
When the wind is snoring,
I'm loving you.
When the day is all you want it to be,
When love is all you see,
I'm loving you.
When nothing seems to flow,
When the day has bumps and you don't know,
I'm loving you.
When the waters are rough,
When pushing through is tough,
I'm loving you.
When the energy is clear,

When you're on task and drawing goodness near,
I'm loving you.
When you know inside
Your passion is alive,
I'm loving you.
The sun will set, and the sun will rise.
Every day is a wonderful surprise.
I'm loving you.
Be the best you.
Be loving to you!

WRITE IT

WRITE IT

WRITE IT

You are every ONE, the one in your decisions to be better or come undone.

EVERYONE

There will be one that enters into your life
There will be one that gives you advice
There will be one that knows better than you
There will be one that figures it out before you do
There will be one challenging your compassion.
There will be one that lives with passion.
There will be one that will influence your way
There will be one that gives good and bad on the same day
There will be one, it's you, that's true
There will be one that pushes you away
There will be one that loves you to stay
There will be one that wants to learn
There will be one that decides it's their turn
There will always be one so you can learn
There will be one that will be triggered by what you do
There will be one that defines you too
There will be one that will go too fast
There will be one that will last
There will be one that pisses you off
There will be one that flips you off
There will be one along life's way every day
There will be one to challenge your way

Everyone can decide who you are and define you from
their own scars
Everyone has to decide to live in front
or behind those bars
You are one of everyone
Sunshine on every one that challenges something
you say or do
The real challenger is the one inside you

WRITE IT

WRITE IT

WRITE IT

Wonder never arrives but instead travels continually through the wilderness with curiosity.

ESSENCE OF WONDER

Let surprise arrive and undertake a search to be alive
Leave adaptation to the conqueror of familiarity
Wonder emerges from the agitation of curiosity
Undertaking possibility and rupturing normalcy
Been there, done that is invalid and unjust to wonder
Create insatiable contemplation into experiencing a jolt
In the expedition into wonder new ideas form
Create a new experience from the wonder
outside of complacency
Walk into the forest of wonder and become the essence

WRITE IT

WRITE IT

Our heart already knows what our mind has not yet disclosed.

HEART IN MOTION

In the randomness of life, emotions are often
spontaneous
We feel from a heart in motion
Rapid change can prompt a rapid heartbeat
Our inner compass and weather changes
without warning
Breathing is treated as a novelty
Until breathing is done with awareness
Our bodies shiver to alert our temperature
Gratitude alerts hope
Pain alerts fight or flight
All of this alerts action
Straight to the heart of it all
Nurture your heart like you'd nurture the tears of a child
Breathe into your life, with heart

WRITE IT

WRITE IT

When we are able to sit in the pain
and in the muck of life,
this is where we see what we
are made of!

BEAUTIFULLY AND
WONDERFULLY MADE

To give honor and respect to another
Honor and respect must first flow through you
To build a secure foundation for oneself inside
Requires tenacity and determination
To love oneself through the highest and lowest of times
Requires oneself to experience love
Love is continually gained and lost before we understand
its significance
Even then there is an unknowing
An unknowing opens up vulnerability
To stand in the muck of life and be vulnerable
That's where we gain our best self
It is where we find what we're made of
Where we get to see where we paid attention
Where we have gone and what we took with us
Shows up

WRITE IT

WRITE IT

Complexity will show up as a blueprint, attempting to define you and your direction. Truth will show up and unravel complexity!

TRUST ME, I'M HERE

My soul's vibration pulls me near
Whispering softly, Trust me, I'm here
Ignite yourself in life, my dear
Take the shackles off your feet and dance
I am here
I am your soul
I am watching you grow
Listen to what you hear
Wear your wild heart without fear
Run and walk
Be still in thought
Clear the traps and release the gaps
They are not meant to last
Surrender to be the best you
Walk past the shadow that darkens what's true
Shine from inside
Your true identity is nothing to hide
Be YOU and live true
We are all what we choose
Sunshine from my heart to you and me too
Love is YOU

WRITE IT

WRITE IT

To listen requires letting go. The heart isn't looking for "who's right or wrong"—that's defense. Listening means that someone else felt the difference between "you heard them" and "they FELT heard."

CENTER OF GRATITUDE

Revel in the invitation to be present
and share your light
Reach and invest in curiosity and devour the
rise to be submerged in joy
The center of gratitude in forgiveness
from pain sustained.

WRITE IT

WRITE IT

The heart shows up without asking.
Do you show up for your heart?

RISK

You must risk the coming and going
of others to grow,
commitment and perseverance
mean saying "NO"
gets easier before saying "Yes"
can gain intention
and wellness!

WRITE IT

WRITE IT

The lesson in the reflection is not seen but heard; it is hidden in the silence of your words!

STRENGTH IN THE CENTER

It is in the voice where the vibration will rise
It is in the stillness when there is a sudden
distraction of surprise
It is in the decision, not the defense, where you discern
Where enlightenment lights the way
Offensive reactions go away
Where understanding is no longer spoken in words
Where trust is as solid as gravity and not considered a verb
Where the human distraction to compress, stress,
and not rest
Is sparked by your persistent best

WRITE IT

WRITE IT

It is within the wave that inspires
both respect and fear. It is within you
to inspire which one you draw near.

PERSEVERE

Where there is truth and love
There will also be a current of the
opposite to gain strength from
In the resistance,
choose perseverance

WRITE IT

Printed in the USA
CPSIA information can be obtained
at www.ICGtesting.com
LVHW042354130124
768898LV00066B/1693